The Usborne
Big Book
of the
Body

Written by Minna Lacey

Illustrated by Peter Allen

Designed by Zuzanna Bukala

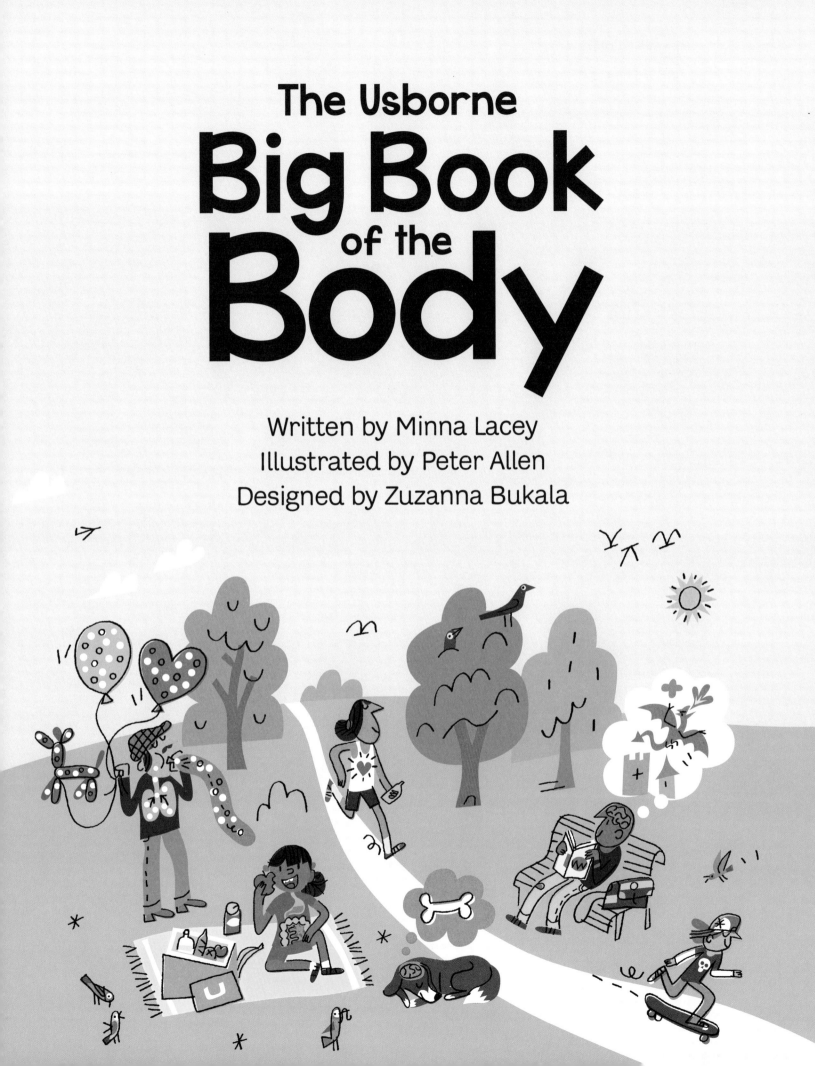

What are you made of?

Your body is made up of lots of different parts – bones, blood, muscles, organs, nerves and skin – all working together to keep you alive and well.

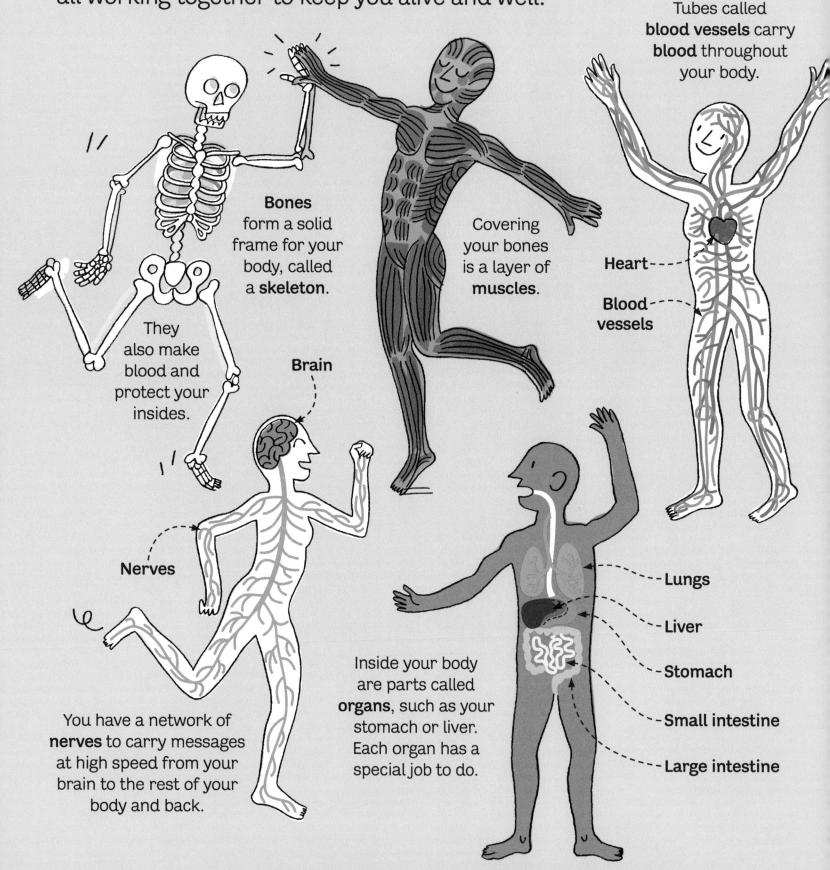

Tubes called **blood vessels** carry **blood** throughout your body.

Bones form a solid frame for your body, called a **skeleton**.

They also make blood and protect your insides.

Covering your bones is a layer of **muscles**.

Heart

Blood vessels

Brain

Nerves

You have a network of **nerves** to carry messages at high speed from your brain to the rest of your body and back.

Inside your body are parts called **organs**, such as your stomach or liver. Each organ has a special job to do.

- - Lungs

- - Liver

- - Stomach

- - Small intestine

- - Large intestine

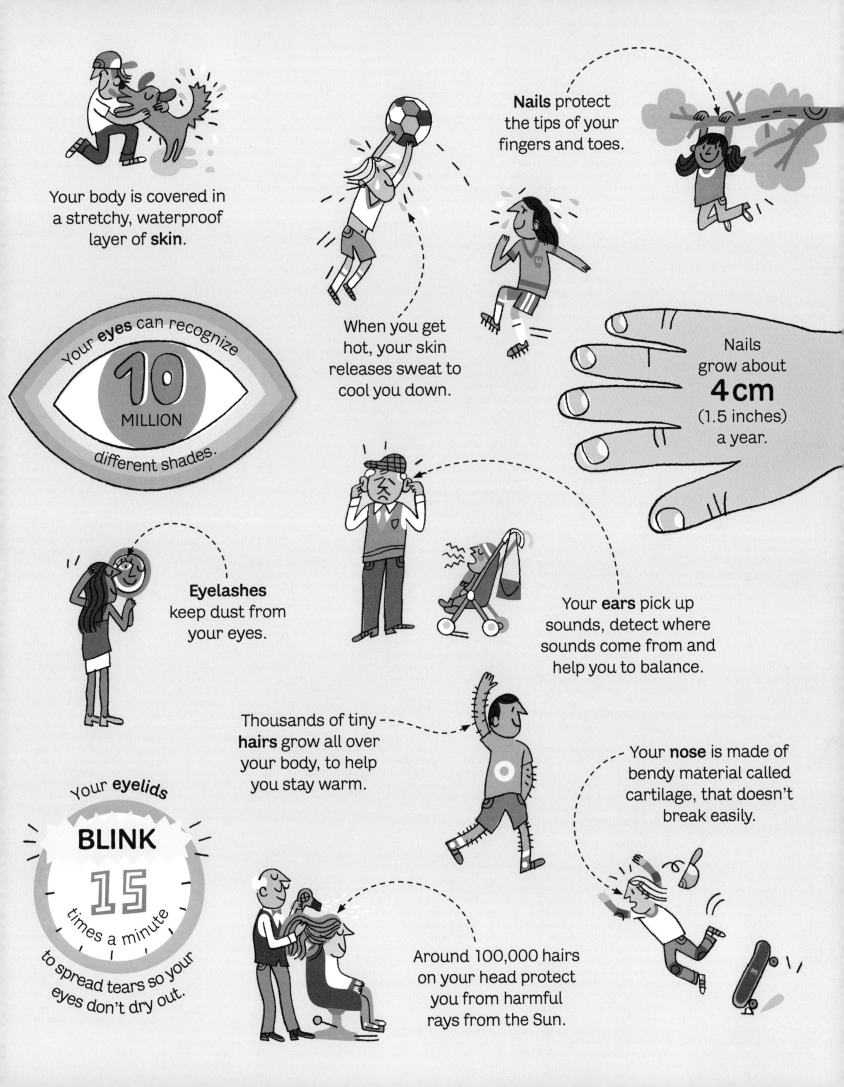

Your body is covered in a stretchy, waterproof layer of **skin**.

Nails protect the tips of your fingers and toes.

When you get hot, your skin releases sweat to cool you down.

Your **eyes** can recognize **10 MILLION** different shades.

Nails grow about **4 cm** (1.5 inches) a year.

Eyelashes keep dust from your eyes.

Your **ears** pick up sounds, detect where sounds come from and help you to balance.

Thousands of tiny **hairs** grow all over your body, to help you stay warm.

Your **nose** is made of bendy material called cartilage, that doesn't break easily.

Your **eyelids** **BLINK** **15** times a minute to spread tears so your eyes don't dry out.

Around 100,000 hairs on your head protect you from harmful rays from the Sun.

Bones

Your bones make a framework, or skeleton, that supports and shapes your body. Some bones help you to move, while others protect your soft body parts.

CAN YOU FEEL...

2 & 3

2 bones in each **THUMB?**

3 bones in each **FINGER?**

Elbow joint

Lower arm bones

The place where two or more bones meet is called a **joint**.

Your **elbow joint** works like a door hinge.

Your **shoulder joint** is shaped like a ball and socket, or cup.

Socket

Ball

Skull

Tap your skull and feel how hard it is.

Your **skull** is shaped like a helmet to protect your brain.

Jaw

Your **eyes** fit into two big round holes in your skull.

Each bone, or group of bones, is shaped for the job it has to do.

Jaw

Thigh bone

Ribs

Skull

Without bones, your body would be all floppy.

Your **jaw** is the only bone you can move in your skull. It allows you to talk, sing and eat.

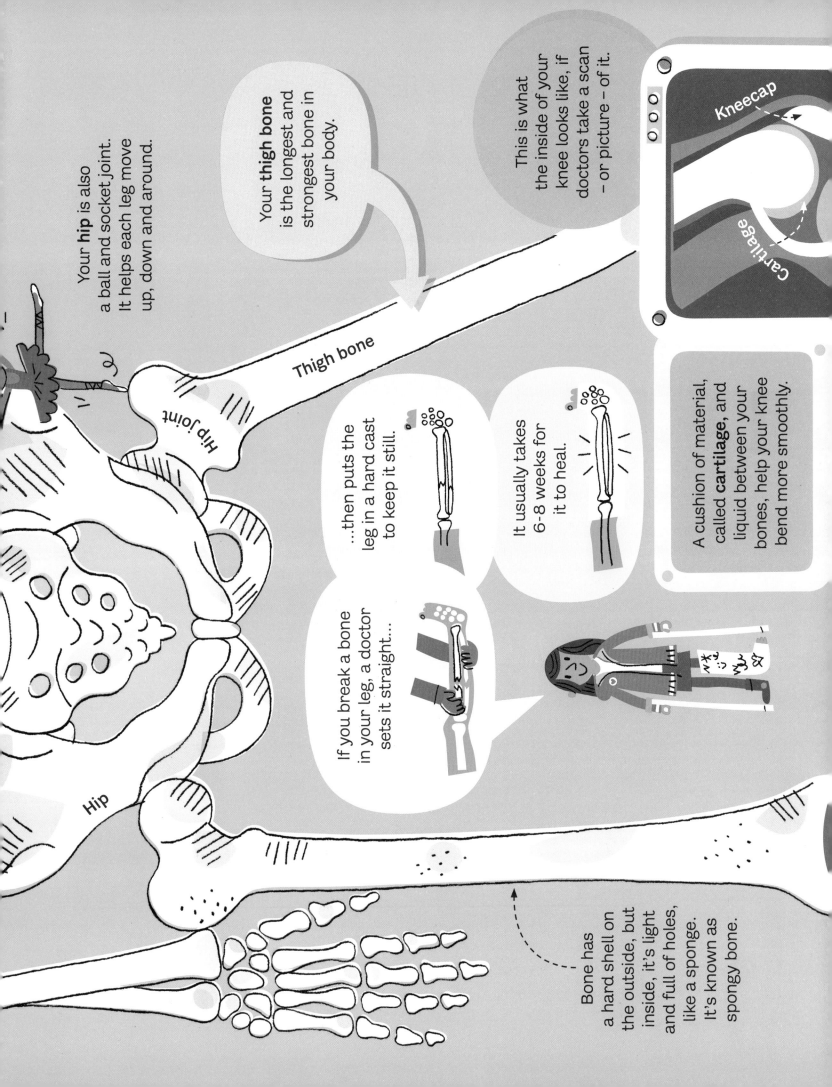

Muscles

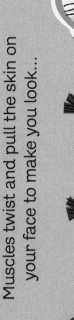

Your muscles are strong and stretchy and pull on different parts of your body. Some are attached to bones and help you to move. Others connect to organs, such as your heart, to help them work.

Muscles twist and pull the skin on your face to make you look...

happy

sad

surprised

cross

confused

scared

You use about **12 MUSCLES** in your face to **SMILE.**

Your jaw muscle is one of the most powerful muscles in your body.

Six muscles connect each eyeball to the skull, so you can move your eyes in different directions.

When you sneeze, your face, throat and chest muscles react suddenly to clear your nose.

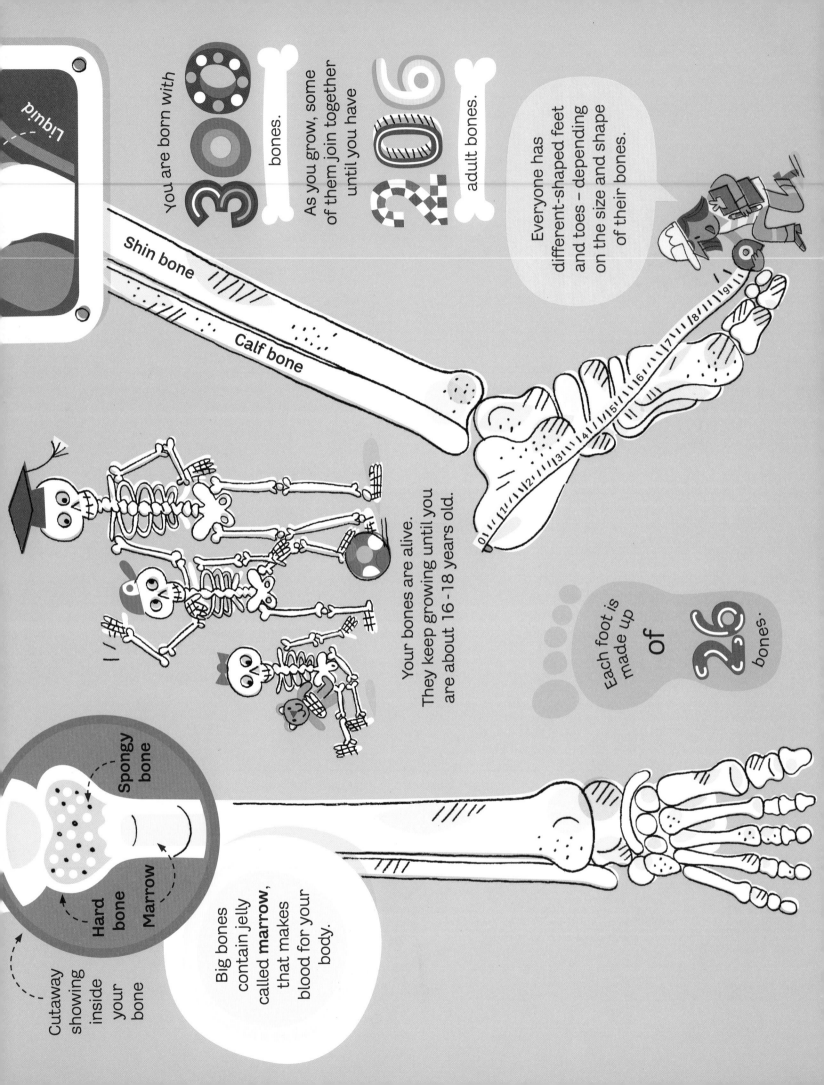

You are born with **300** bones.

As you grow, some of them join together until you have **206** adult bones.

Shin bone

Calf bone

Everyone has different-shaped feet and toes – depending on the size and shape of their bones.

Liquid

Your bones are alive. They keep growing until you are about 16 - 18 years old.

Each foot is made up of **26** bones.

Cutaway showing inside your bone

Spongy bone

Hard bone

Marrow

Big bones contain jelly called **marrow**, that makes blood for your body.

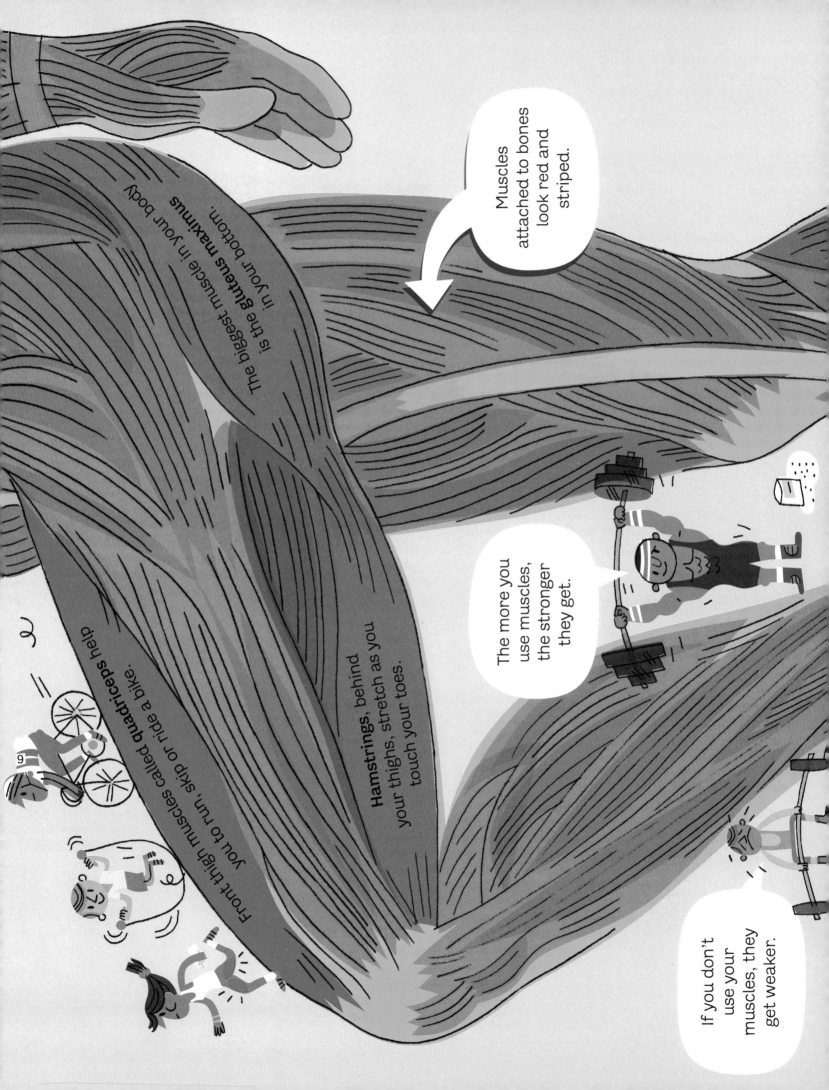

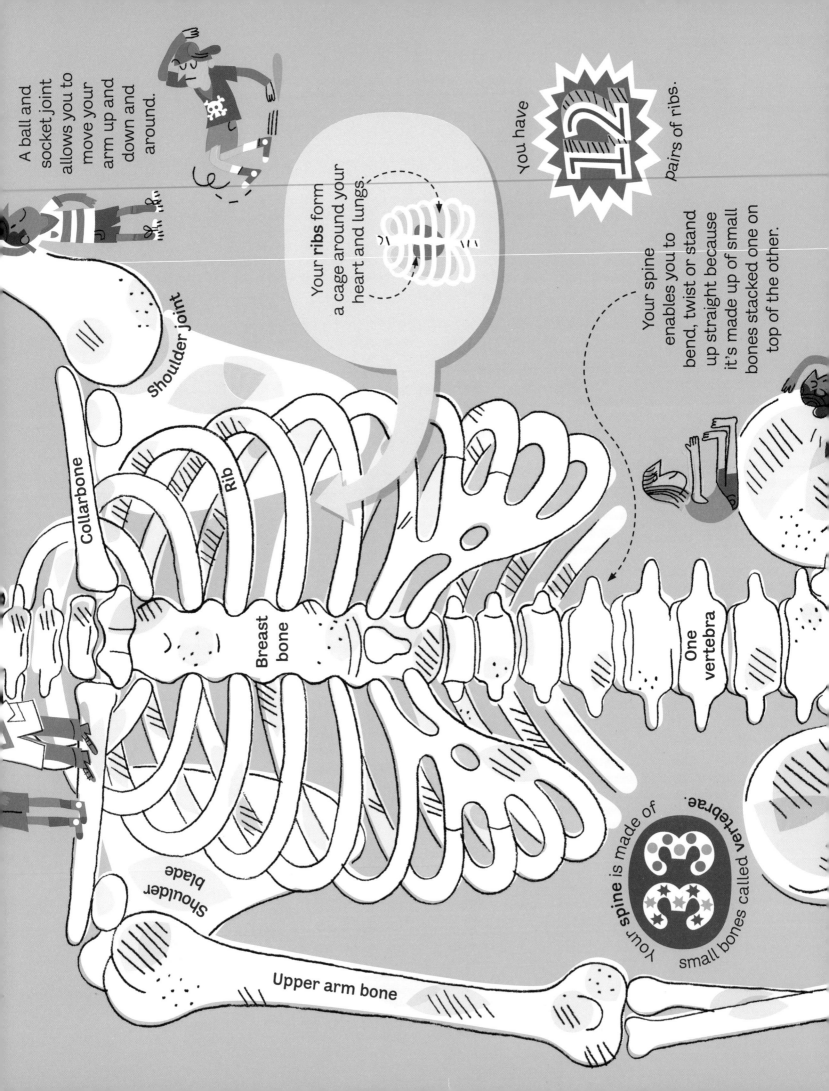

A ball and socket joint allows you to move your arm up and down and around.

Your **ribs** form a cage around your heart and lungs.

You have

12

pairs of ribs.

Your spine enables you to bend, twist or stand up straight because it's made up of small bones stacked one on top of the other.

Shoulder joint

Collarbone

Rib

Breast bone

One vertebra

Shoulder blade

Upper arm bone

Your **spine** is made of

33

small bones called **vertebrae**.

Taking a breath

When you breathe in, your lungs fill with air which contains a gas called oxygen. Your body needs oxygen to stay alive.

Oxygen is in the air, but it's also in all parts of your body.

Muscles

Bones

Teeth

Blood

Plants, trees and animals need oxygen to live and grow too.

Lungs are soft and spongy with lots of tubes for air to pass through.

Right lung

A large muscle called the **diaphragm** helps you to breathe.

- - - - **Lungs**

- - **Diaphragm**

Your diaphragm moves down to draw air into your lungs.

Your diaphragm moves up to push air out of your lungs.

Your left lung is slightly smaller – to leave room for your heart.

Diaphragm

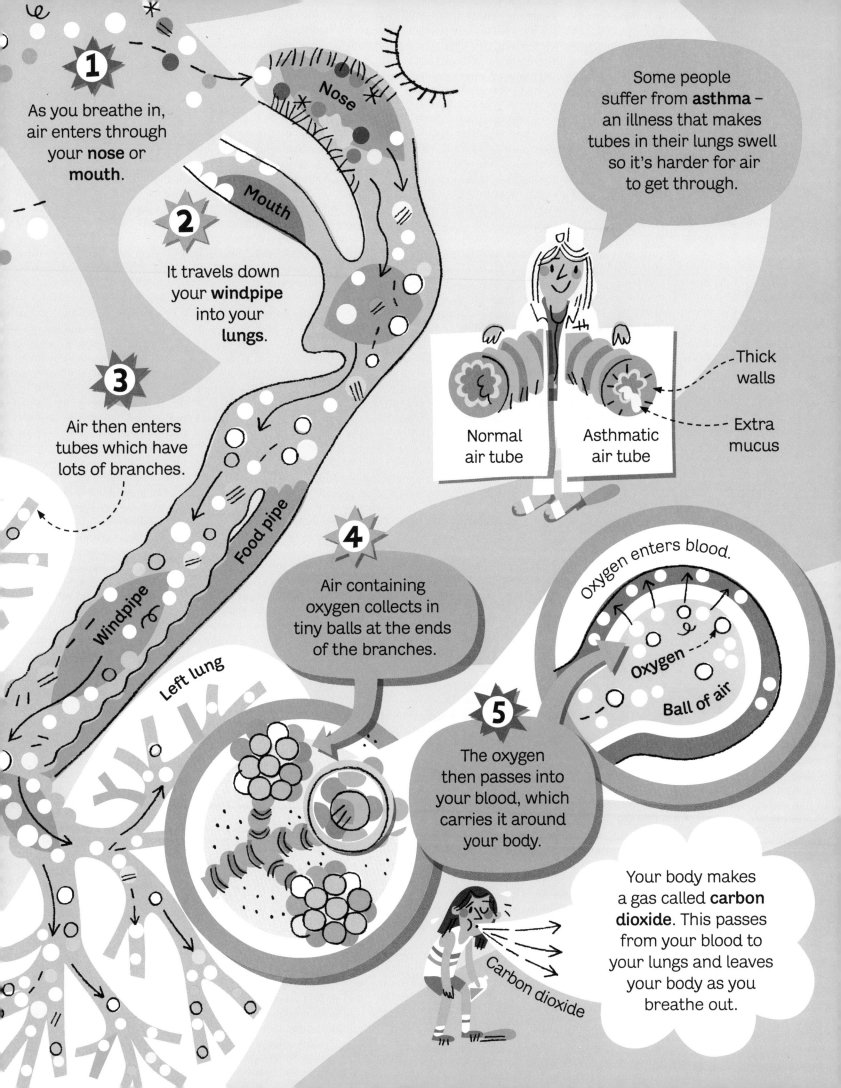

Heart and blood

Your heart pumps blood all around your body – up to your head and down to the tips of your fingers and toes.

Your heart is like two separate pumps that work together.

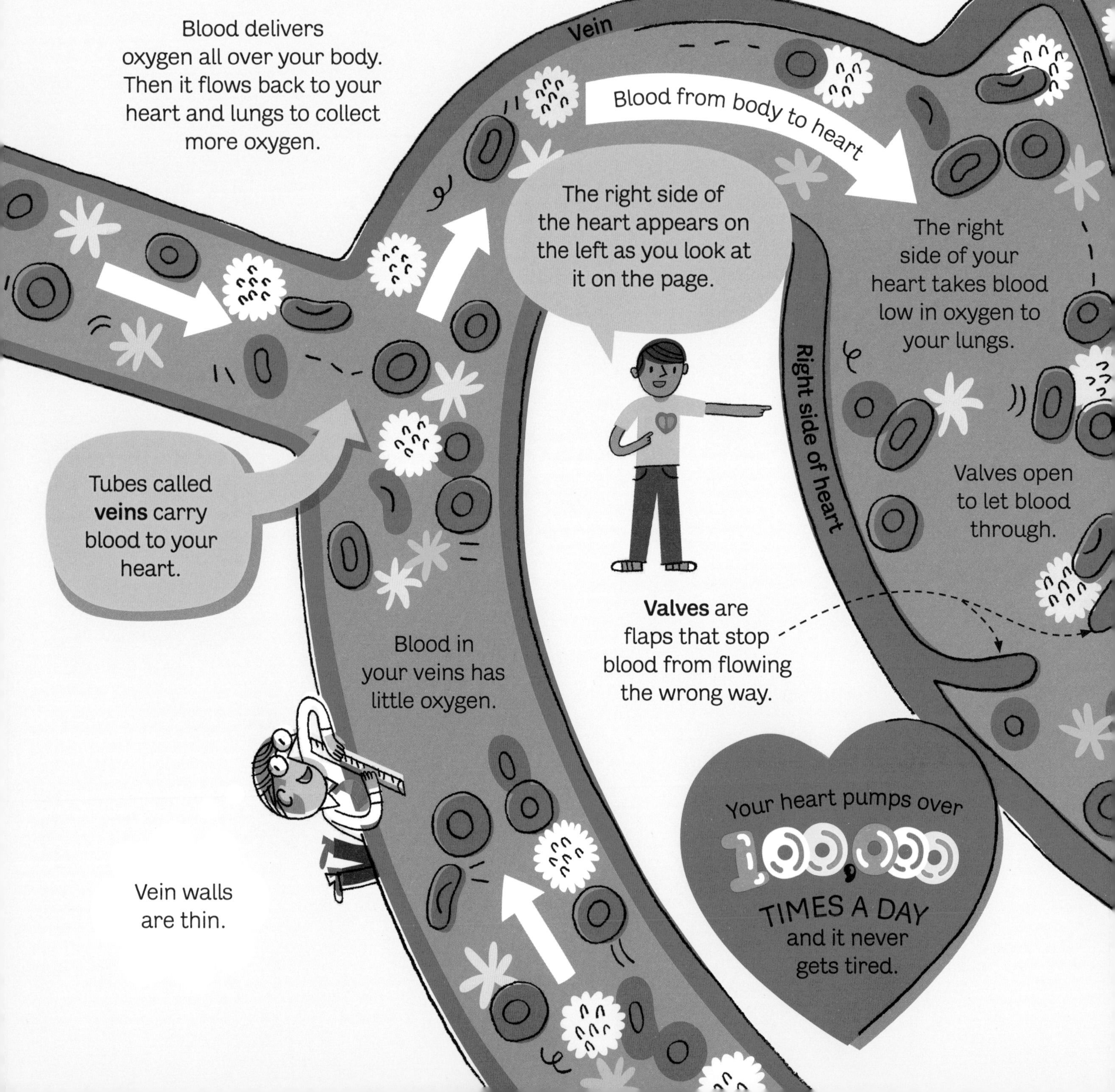

To lungs

Blood delivers oxygen all over your body. Then it flows back to your heart and lungs to collect more oxygen.

Vein

Blood from body to heart

The right side of the heart appears on the left as you look at it on the page.

The right side of your heart takes blood low in oxygen to your lungs.

Right side of heart

Tubes called **veins** carry blood to your heart.

Valves open to let blood through.

Blood in your veins has little oxygen.

Valves are flaps that stop blood from flowing the wrong way.

Vein walls are thin.

Your heart pumps over 100,000,000 TIMES A DAY and it never gets tired.

Artery

To body

From lungs

Left side of heart

To body

To lungs

Blood collects here, then is pumped to the lungs.

Your heart is roughly the size of your closed fist.

The left side of your heart takes blood full of oxygen from your lungs to the rest of your body.

The left side is stronger because it has to pump hard to make the blood reach every part of your body.

Tubes called **arteries** carry blood from your heart around your body.

Artery walls are thicker.

Blood in your arteries is full of oxygen and looks brighter.

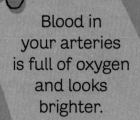

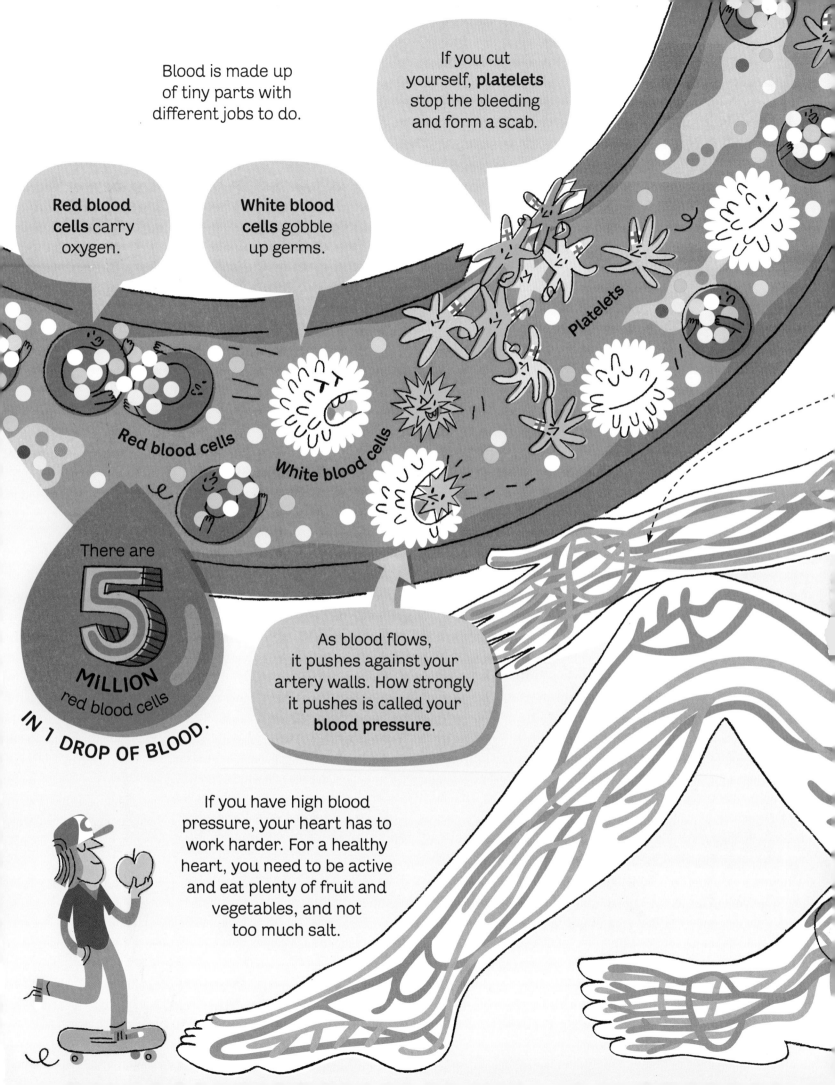

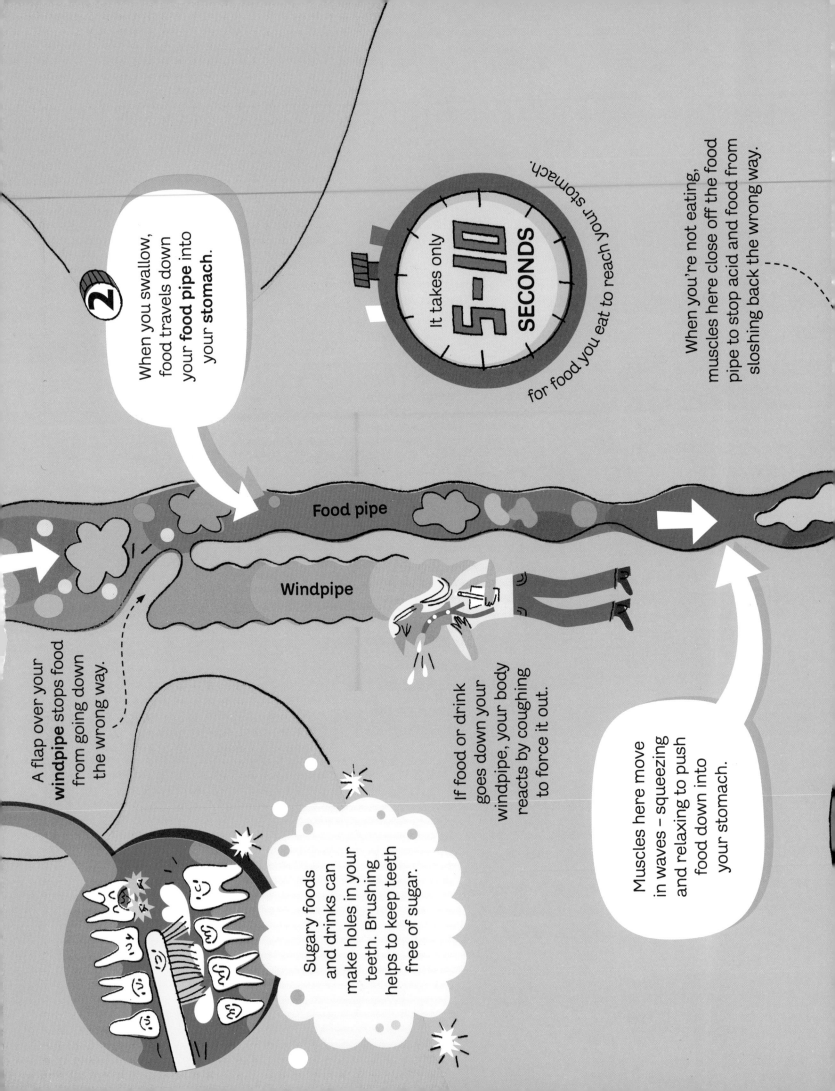

Where does your food go?

When you eat, food goes on a long twisty journey, zigzagging through tubes and turning into a soupy mush for your body to use.

Food gives you energy and helps you grow and stay healthy.

A good balance of different types of food helps you feel and look good.

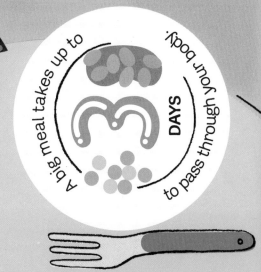

A big meal takes up to **3 DAYS** to pass through your body.

Your **saliva** - spit - starts to dissolve food and makes it easier to swallow.

Your **tongue** pushes small pieces of food to the back of your mouth.

1 Your **teeth** cut, grind and chew food into small pieces.

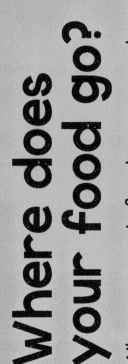

Blood flows through a giant network of arteries and veins.

As your heart pumps, blood flows in tiny bursts called **pulses**. You can sometimes feel this on the inside of your wrist or your neck.

Your heart beats faster when you're nervous or scared.

This prepares you for danger, in case you need to run away or defend yourself.

Blood flows faster when you run, to get more oxygen to your muscles.

When you are asleep, you need less oxygen, so your heart beats more slowly.

Large thigh vein

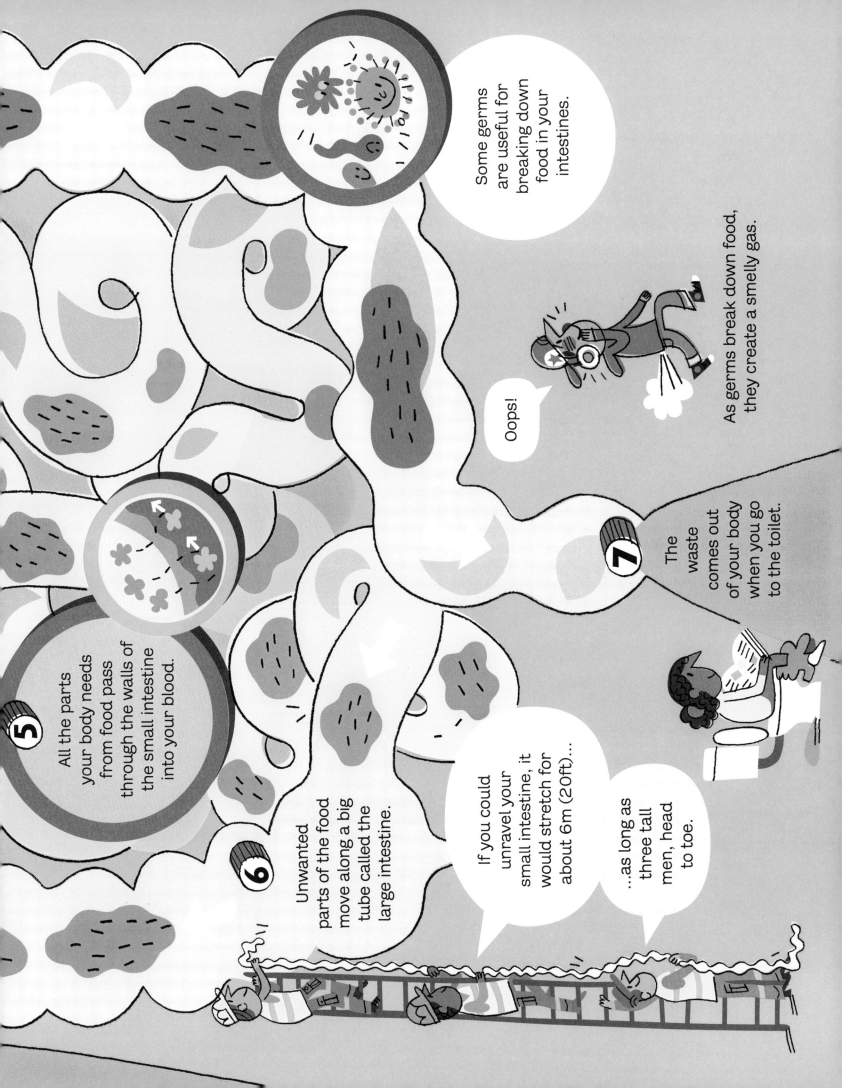

Inside your head

Your brain controls almost everything you do. It works by constantly sending and receiving messages, and allows you to think, move and sense the world around you.

This picture shows the left side of your brain.

Different areas of your brain control different activities. The areas are shaded here to help show you where they are.

Touch

Movement

Complicated movement

Taste

Talking

Smell

Thinking

Liquid

Skull

Memory and emotion

Your brain works all the time, even when you are asleep.

Your skull, three coverings and a cushion of liquid protect your brain from bumps.

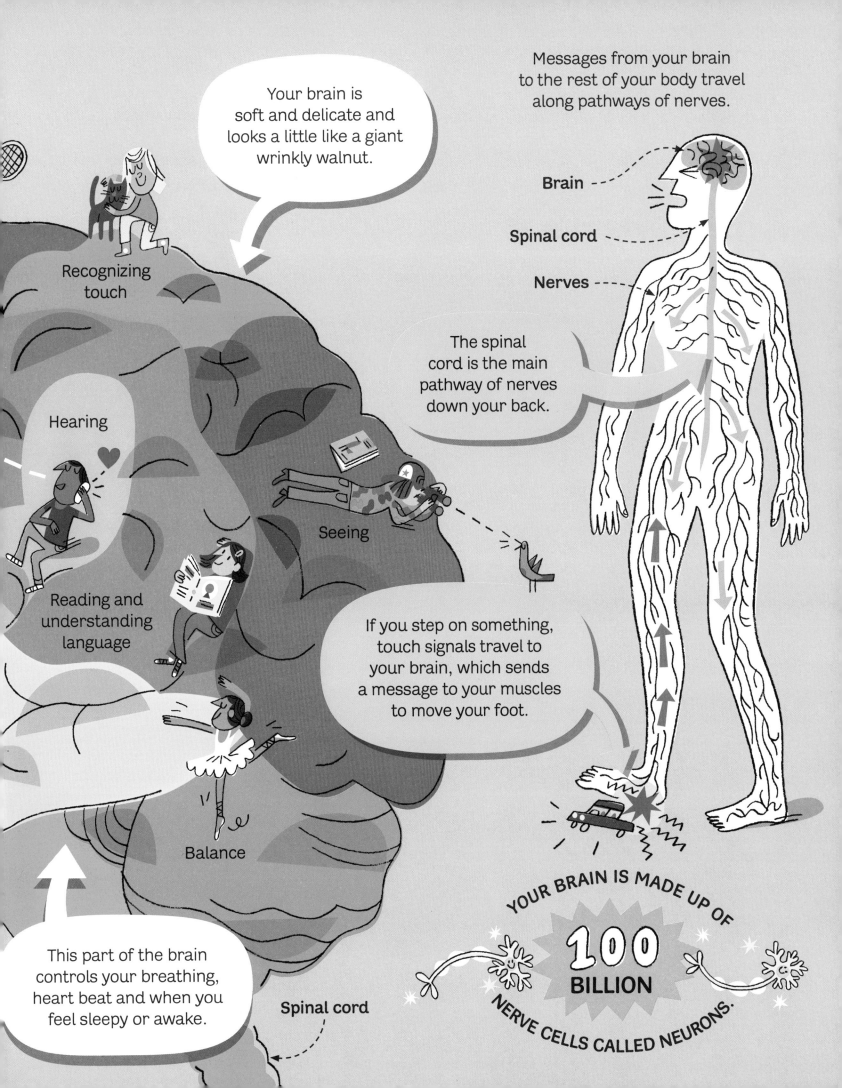

Your senses

Five main senses – seeing, hearing, touch, taste and smell – send information to your brain about what's happening around you.

Touch

Your **skin** contains millions of receptors that detect touch and send signals to your brain.

Smell

Smells are chemicals released into the air by things, such as flowers, cheese and dirty socks.

Receptors also detect whether something is hot, cold or painful.

They enter your nose as you breathe in.

Smell is linked to memory, and can remind you of things long ago.

Hairs

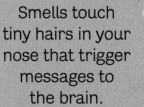

Smells touch tiny hairs in your nose that trigger messages to the brain.

Taste

Your mouth is full of taste sensors called **tastebuds**, found mostly in tiny bumps on your tongue.

Tastebuds detect four main types of food: salty, bitter, sour and sweet.

Taste can stop you from eating food that's gone bad.

Feeling pain warns you that something is wrong. If you hurt yourself, pain makes you stop and get help.

Hearing

Your ears pick up thousands of different sounds – from rustling leaves and twangy guitars to the hoot of an owl.

1 Sounds travel in waves through the air.

2 Sounds pass through a layer of skin, called an **ear drum**, to three tiny bones and a spiral tube...

Woo
woo

Rustle
Rustle

Twang
Twang

Ear drum

Three bones

Spiral tube

3 ...which sends signals to the brain.

Seeing

You see something because light shines on it, then bounces off it into your eyes.

1 Light enters your eye through a hole called the **pupil**. It passes through a **lens** to the back of your eyeball...

2 ...where images form upside down.

3 Your brain turns the images the right way up.

Brain

Light rays

Pupil

Lens

Wide pupils

Your pupils are the black dots in the middle of your eyes. They open and close to let in more or less light.

Narrow pupils

If your own lenses don't work properly, you can correct them with glasses.

Starting life

It takes about nine months for a baby to grow inside its mother – then it's ready to be born. Many changes take place as children grow into adults.

First a tiny **sperm** from a man joins with a tiny **egg** from a woman.

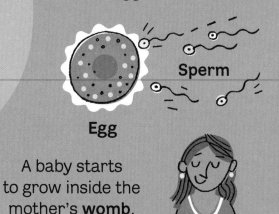

Sperm

Egg

A baby starts to grow inside the mother's **womb**.

Womb

An unborn baby stays safe inside a pouch of liquid. It gets food and oxygen from its mother through a tube.

After two months, it's about the size and shape of a kidney bean.

By six months, the baby can yawn, kick and hear sounds outside the womb.

At about nine months, the baby is born. A new baby grows fast.

By one year, a baby weighs roughly **3** times its weight at birth.

Children keep growing and changing, until finally they become adults.

Most babies are born with no teeth.

From around six months, your baby teeth begin to show.

From six years, adult teeth start pushing out the baby teeth one by one – until you have 32 adult teeth.

See if you can answer the questions to this quiz.

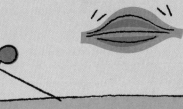

Body quiz

1. How many bones do you have in each foot?

2. How many bones are there in an adult body?

3. What is the biggest muscle in your body?

4. What gas do you breathe in through your lungs?

5. Which side of your heart is stronger?

6. What are your five main senses?

You can find the answers by looking back through the book.

With expert advice from Dr. Kristina Routh
Series designer: Laura Wood   Series editor: Jane Chisholm

On the internet
You can find out more about the human body by going to www.usborne.com/quicklinks
and typing in the keywords **big book of the body**. We recommend
that children are supervised while on the internet.

Answers:
1. 26; 2. 206; 3. Gluteus maximus; 4. Oxygen; 5. The left side;
6. Seeing, hearing, touch, taste and smell.